DECORATING
COOKIES

DECORATING
COOKIES

Joanna Farrow

Watson-Guptill Publications
New York

First published in the United States
in 2001 by Watson-Guptill Publications
a division of BPI Communications, Inc.
770 Broadway, New York, NY 10003
www.watsonguptill.com

Commissioning Editor: Barbara Croxford
Design & Art Direction: Fay Singer
Project Editor: Angela Newton
Photographer: Craig Robertson
Stylist: Penny Markham
CEO: Robert Oerton
Publisher: Catie Ziller
Publishing Manager: Fia Fornari
Production Manager: Lucy Byrne
Group General Manager: Mark Smith
Group CEO/Publisher: Anne Wilson

Library of Congress Catalog
Card Number: 00-109231
ISBN 0-8230-1266-2

First published in the United Kingdom
in 2000 by Merehurst Limited
an imprint of
Murdoch Books (UK) Ltd
Ferry House, 51–57 Lacy Road,
Putney, London, SW15 1PR

Color separation by Colourscan, Singapore
Printed in Singapore by Tien Wah Press

First printing, 2001
1 2 3 4 5 6 7 8 9 / 07 06 05 04 03 02 01

Contents

Introduction

The art of cookie decoration has been practiced for centuries, dating back to when spicy gingerbreads were gilded with gold paint, studded with whole spices, or baked in elaborate molds to enhance their appearance. In this book, the idea has been developed to cover a wealth of different decorative techniques – some simple and instantly achievable, others rather more intricate and time consuming.

Some of the designs have a distinctly seasonal theme, while others are perfect for more specific occasions such as weddings, christenings, and birthdays. Many of the shapes can be used as eyecatching decorations, or even as attractive, personalized gifts. Appealing to adults and children alike, these cookies are sure to be as much fun to make as they are to receive.

Recipes

Dark gingerbread

3¼ cups self-rising flour

2 teaspoons ground ginger

½ teaspoon ground cloves

½ cup firm unsalted butter

⅔ cup dark brown sugar

⅓ cup molasses

1 egg, lightly beaten

makes about 24

preparation time 10 minutes, plus chilling time

baking time 12–15 minutes

1 Preheat the oven to 400°F and grease two cookie sheets thoroughly.

2 Put the flour and spices in a food processor. Cut the butter into small pieces, add to the processor, and blend until the mixture resembles breadcrumbs. Add the sugar, molasses, and egg, and mix to a dough. Wrap and chill for at least 30 minutes.

3 Roll out the mixture on a floured surface. Cut out rounds or squares and place on the cookie sheets. Bake for 12–15 minutes until the shapes have risen slightly and appear a little paler in color. Leave for 2 minutes, then transfer to a wire rack to cool.

Light gingerbread

3 cups all-purpose flour

2 teaspoons baking powder

2 teaspoons ground ginger

scant ½ cup firm unsalted butter

1 cup light brown sugar

3 tablespoons corn syrup

1 egg, lightly beaten

makes about 24

preparation time 10 minutes, plus chilling time

baking time 12 minutes

1 Preheat the oven to 400°F and grease two cookie sheets thoroughly.

2 Put the flour, baking powder, and ginger in a food processor. Cut the butter into small pieces, add to the food processor, and blend until the mixture resembles breadcrumbs. Add the sugar, syrup, and egg, and blend to a dough. Wrap and chill for at least 30 minutes.

3 Roll out the mixture on a floured surface. Cut out rounds or squares and place on the cookie sheets. Bake for about 12 minutes until the shapes turn golden around the edges. Leave for 2 minutes, then transfer to a wire rack to cool.

Butter cookies

2¼ cups all-purpose flour

⅞ cup firm unsalted butter

⅘ cup confectioners' sugar

2 egg yolks

1 teaspoon vanilla extract

(For chocolate butter cookies, substitute ¼ cup cocoa powder for ¼ cup of the flour.)

makes about 20

preparation time 10 minutes, plus chilling time

baking time 6–10 minutes

1 Preheat the oven to 400°F and grease two cookie sheets thoroughly.

2 Put the flour in a food processor. Cut the butter into small pieces, add it to the food processor, and blend together until the mixture resembles breadcrumbs. Add the sugar, egg yolks, and vanilla extract and blend to a smooth dough. Wrap and chill for an hour.

3 Roll out the mixture on a floured surface, cut out rounds or squares, and place on the cookie sheets. Bake for about 6–10 minutes until the pieces turn golden around the edges. Transfer the plain or chocolate butter cookie shapes to a wire rack to cool.

Icing glaze (single quantity)

1 egg white

1 tablespoon lemon juice

1¼ cups confectioners' sugar, sifted

preparation time 3 minutes

1 Lightly whisk the egg white and lemon juice in a bowl.

2 Gradually whisk in the confectioners' sugar until the mixture has a smooth texture and is the consistency of a pouring cream.

3 Cover the surface of the icing with plastic wrap to prevent a crust from forming until ready for use.

Royal icing (single quantity)

1 egg white

approx 1¾ cups confectioners' sugar, sifted

preparation time 3 minutes

1 Lightly whisk the egg white in a bowl. Gradually whisk in a sufficient quantity of confectioners' sugar to make a softly peaking icing.

2 Cover the surface of the icing with plastic wrap to prevent a crust from forming until ready for use.

Basic techniques

Working with cookie dough

Cookie dough is generally easy to work with, even for inexperienced cooks. If you follow a few simple guidelines, cookies can be made and baked effortlessly, ready for the enjoyment of decorating.

1 Once the cookie mixture is made, either in the food processor or by hand, it must be chilled for at least 30 minutes – preferably longer – to firm up. Otherwise the mixture can be too soft to work with and will easily lose its shape during baking. For this reason, you may prefer to make it in advance. Store the dough, wrapped in plastic wrap or foil, for up to two days. It also freezes well for up to 1 month.

2 Cut out the shapes and position the pieces on the cookie sheet. Allow space between each cookie as the pieces will expand slightly during baking.

3 For larger cookie shapes, such as the gingerbread cottage on page 90, you may find it easier to cut out the shapes on the cookie sheet so they do not distort as you transfer them from the work surface.

4 Rather than waste leftover dough, reroll and bake the trimmings. They are good for practicing decorative techniques and, of course, taste good un-iced!

5 For hanging cookie always remember to re-mark the holes after baking because the dough will have expanded slightly on cooking. Do this as soon as the cookies come out of the oven, while they are still soft.

6 Due to the high sugar content, all cookies are soft when they first come out of the oven. Therefore, do not be tempted to bake them for extra time – they will quickly turn crisp on cooling. Leave the cookies on the cookie sheets to cool slightly before transferring them to the wire cooling rack, to prevent them from falling apart.

Icing and rolled fondant

Royal icing is easy to make and perfect for piping decorations. Do not make the consistency too stiff, otherwise it will be difficult to squeeze through the small tips. Incorporate the confectioners' sugar until the icing is softly peaking, rather than stiff.

Cake-decorating supply stores stock a wide range of rolled fondant colors while supermarkets usually only sell a few basic ones. If you just need a small quantity of several colors, buy a small pack of white rolled fondant and knead in the appropriate colors. Generally, paste colors give the richest tones while liquid ones produce more pastel shades.

All icings can be prepared a day in advance and stored in a cool place or in the refrigerator. For royal icing and icing glaze, cover the actual surface with plastic wrap, and keep rolled fondant tightly wrapped in plastic wrap or foil to prevent a crust from forming.

Making a paper piping bag

Paper piping bags are particularly useful for decorating as the tip can be snipped off, thus removing the need for a metal tip. (However, metal tips are useful for piping intricate shapes because a snipped paper tip does not always pipe perfect lines.) Paper bags are also disposable, of course, hence no and washing up!

1 Cut a 7½in square of baking parchment in half diagonally, creating two triangles.

2 Holding one triangle with the longest side away from you, curl the left-hand point over to meet the point nearest you, shaping a cone.

3 Curl the right-hand point over the cone, bringing the points neatly together. Then fold the points over several times to secure the bag in place.

Fan-assisted ovens

Remember that fan-assisted ovens should be set at lower temperatures than conventional ovens – a general rule is 70ºF cooler than the temperature stated.

Using templates

Many of the cookie designs require one or more of the templates on pages 124–126. Baking parchment can be used although a plain sheet of paper tends to be easier to work with. Rest the template on the rolled out dough and cut carefully around it. For basic shapes, a small, sharp knife is usually adequate. For more intricate shapes, an X-acto knife tends to be easier to manage.

Melting chocolate

Melted semisweet, milk, or white chocolate can be used for coating cookies or for piping decorations.

1 Break the chocolate into small, even-sized pieces and put it in a heatproof bowl.

2 Place the bowl over a small pan of very gently simmering water and leave the chocolate to melt. Make sure the base of the bowl does not touch the water or the chocolate will overheat.

3 Stir gently to check that no lumps remain before use.

TIP Chocolate can also be melted in the microwave. Break up the chocolate into a bowl and allow 1½–2 minutes for 3oz chocolate. Leave to stand for a minute then stir gently. Microwave again if lumps remain.

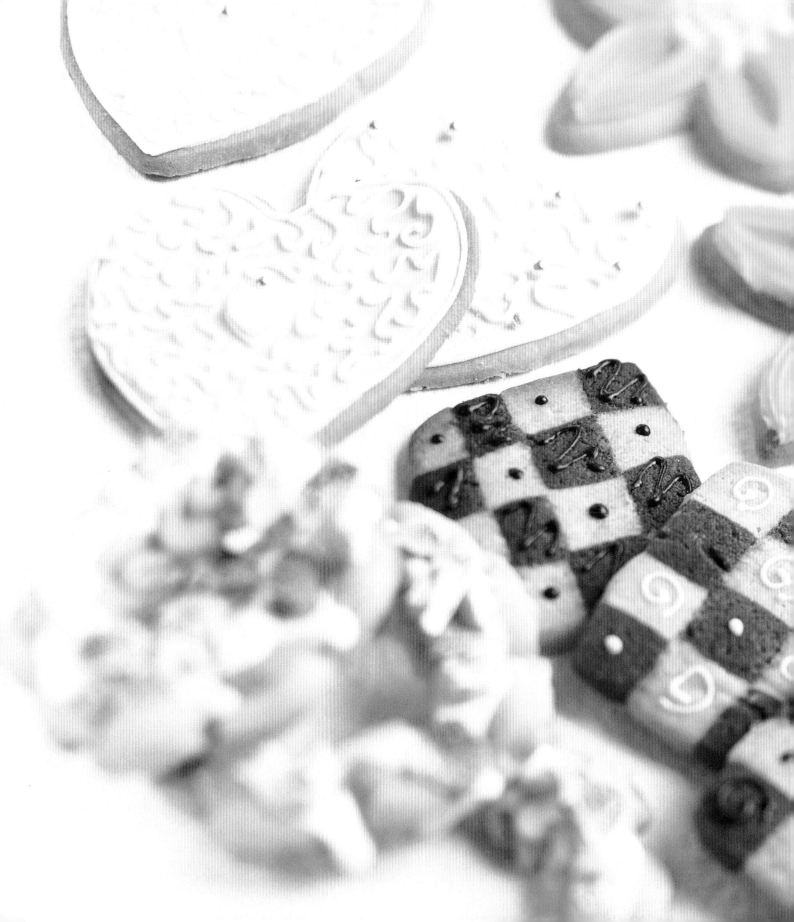

Springtime

Flower garlands

Unlike most doughs, this mixture is piped rather than rolled out. It does require patience to pipe the garlands – but the results are well worth the effort.

1 Preheat the oven to 350°F and grease the two cookie sheets. Mix together the butter and superfine sugar, to form a very pale, creamy paste. Add the flour and lemon juice and stir to a smooth mixture. Transfer the paste to a piping bag fitted with a large star writing tip. (You might find it easier to add only half the mixture, and top the bag up with more mixture as you work.)

2 Pipe rings of small scallops on to the cookie sheets so that each one just touches the next. Twist the end of the

¾ cup unsalted butter, softened
¼ cup superfine sugar
2 cups all-purpose flour
4 teaspoons lemon juice
icing and decoration
¼ cup superfine sugar
small amount of lightly beaten egg white
several miniature roses
12 white or colored sugared almonds
1¼ cups confectioners' sugar, sifted
6–8 teaspoons lemon juice or rosewater

equipment
2 cookie sheets
large nylon piping bag
½in star writing tip
wire cooling rack
plastic bag
paintbrush
rolling pin
makes 12
baking time 12 minutes

bag firmly after piping each shape. Bake the garlands for about 12 minutes until they turn a pale, golden color. Leave the garlands to stand on the cookie sheets for 2 minutes to harden and cool slightly, before transferring them to a wire cooling rack.

3 To make the sugared rose petals, put the superfine sugar and egg white in separate small containers. Remove the petals from one of the miniature roses. Coat both sides of one of the rose petals with a small amount of egg white. (Use a paintbrush for coating the petal, or simply rub the surface with your thumb and forefinger dipped in the egg white.)

4 Sprinkle the petal surfaces with superfine sugar and place them on a sheet of paper to dry. Repeat this process for the other petals – you will need about five petals for each of the garlands.

5 Put the sugared almonds in a plastic bag and lightly beat them with the end of a rolling pin to break the nuts into small pieces.

6 Stir together the confectioners' sugar and lemon juice or rosewater, to create a smooth mixture. Use the small teaspoon to drizzle a modest quantity of icing over each of the garlands.

7 While the icing is still soft, arrange some of the sugared rose petals over each garland. Gently press them into the icing. Arrange the broken pieces of sugared almonds between the petals. Put the garlands aside to set for 1–2 hours. Then store the shapes in an airtight container for up to two days, stacking them no more than two deep. Interleave layers of baking parchment between the garlands, to help prevent them from sticking.

TIPS Make sure the butter you use is really soft before creaming it with the sugar, otherwise it will be very difficult to pipe from the bag. It is best to leave the butter at room temperature for several hours or microwave it briefly.

Once sugared, the rose petals should keep for several weeks in a cool, dry place, enabling you to make them well in advance.

Miniature roses are just the right size for decorating cookies but you could use any other small, edible flowers that are on hand. Tiny primroses and violets are particularly effective, and small herb flowers are an unusual, attractive variation.

If you are very short on preparation time, you could always buy tiny crystallized roses or violets from a supermarket or cake-decorating supplier.

Valentine's Day hearts

These pretty, piped hearts, with their different designs, make ideal decorations for Valentine's Day, engagement, wedding, or anniversary celebrations.

1 Preheat the oven to 400°F and grease the two cookie sheets. Roll out the butter cookie mixture on a floured surface and use the large cookie cutter to cut out the hearts. Transfer them to the cookie sheet and bake for 8 minutes or until they turn golden around the edges. Leave on the cookie sheets for 2 minutes, then transfer them to a wire rack to cool.

2 Using a metal spatula, spread the icing glaze over the hearts. Try to achieve a thin, even layer, spreading the icing just to the edges of the shapes.

butter cookie mixture (see page 9)
icing and decoration
icing glaze (see page 9)
1³⁄₄oz white rolled fondant
confectioners' sugar for dusting
royal icing (see page 9)
silver dragées
equipment
2 cookie sheets
rolling pin
3in and ¹⁄₂in heart-shaped cookie cutters

wire cooling rack
metal spatula
paper piping bag
medium writing tip
makes 16–18
baking time 8 minutes

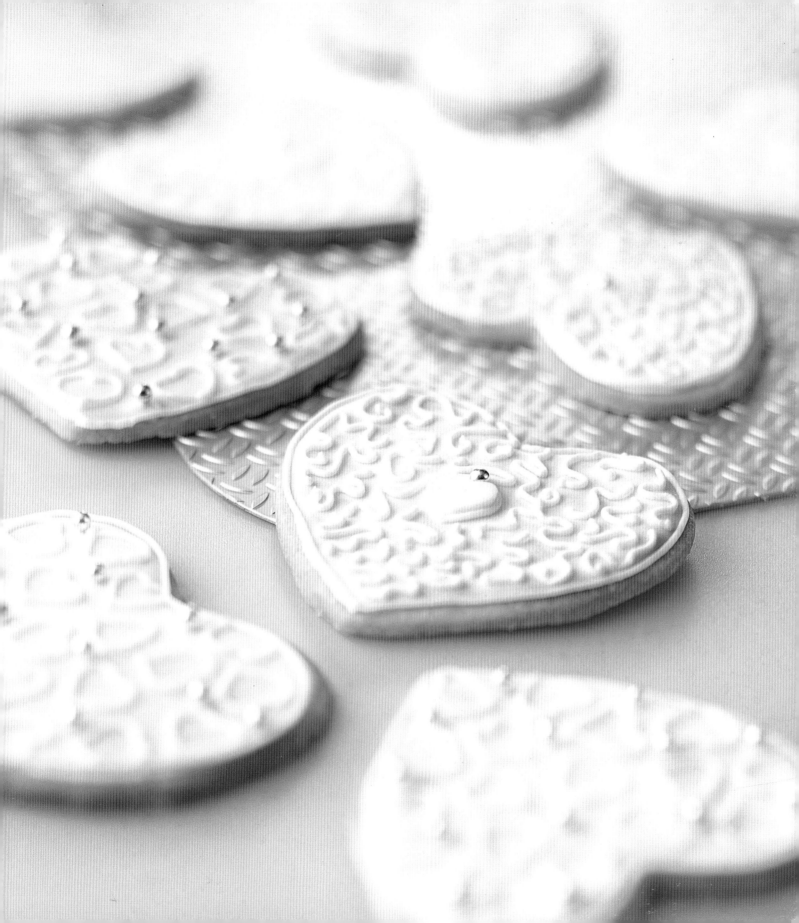

3 Thinly roll the fondant on a surface dusted with confectioners' sugar. Cut out heart shapes from the rolled fondant, using the small cookie cutter.

4 Put the royal icing in a piping bag fitted with a medium writing tip. Pipe a small amount of icing in the center of about half of the cookies. Position the rolled fondant hearts over the icing and secure them in place. Leave aside for about 30 minutes until touch dry.

5 Use the small cookie cutter to impress heart shapes into the icing on the remaining cookies. Leave about ¼in between each heart and adjust the angles of each.

6 Pipe a line around the edge of each cookie, then pipe lines around the edges of the single-heart cookies and secure a dragée at the top of each. Pipe decorative wavy filigree lines all over the glaze.

7 Pipe over the impressed lines on the remaining cookies to accentuate the heart shapes and secure dragées at intervals between the hearts, securing each with a dot of icing from the bag.

TIP For added decoration, make holes near the tops of the hearts before baking so that they can be threaded with ribbons, which can then be tied in bows.

Mother's Day flowers

A plain, round cookie cutter is all you need to shape these simple flower cookies, unless, of course, you have a similarly shaped flower cookie cutter.

1 Preheat the oven to 400°F. Grease two cookie sheets. Roll out the butter cookie mixture on a floured surface and cut into 1in wide strips.

2 Using the cookie cutter, cut out semicircular shapes from the strips, then cut out the straight side from each semicircle to make petal shapes (see overleaf).

3 Arrange a petal on the cookie sheet and brush the tip with a little lightly beaten egg white. Position another petal over the top and press down gently to secure. Arrange

butter cookie mixture (see page 9)
small amount of lightly beaten egg white
icing and decoration
scant ½ cup unsalted butter, softened
1¾ cups confectioners' sugar, sifted
green and yellow food coloring
equipment
2 cookie sheets
3in round cookie cutter
wire cooling rack
paper piping bags

small star tip
makes 16–18
baking time 8 minutes

three more petals to assemble a complete flower, brushing the end of each with egg white. Assemble the remaining flowers in the same way. Reroll the trimmings to make more flowers.

Bake for about 8 minutes until they turn a pale, golden color around the edges. Leave on the cookie sheets for 5 minutes, then transfer to a wire rack to cool.

To make the buttercream, beat the butter in a bowl until soft. Add the confectioners' sugar and beat well until pale and creamy, adding a few drops of boiling water if necessary to make creaming easier.

Spoon a quarter of the mixture into a piping bag and snip off the tip. Spoon another quarter into a bowl and color it pale green. Feed this into another piping bag and snip off the tip. Color the remaining buttercream pale yellow and feed into a bag fitted with a star tip.

Use the yellow buttercream to pipe around the edges of the petals, keeping clear of the centers of the flowers.

Use the buttercream in the other two piping bags to pipe dots into the centers of the flowers. Leave aside to firm up before storing the shapes in a container layered with baking parchment.

Chocolate checkerboard

These buttery, two-tone squares are easy to shape and the contrast is extremely effective. The melted chocolate adds a perfect finishing touch.

1 Preheat the oven to 400°F and lightly grease the large cookie sheet. On a floured surface, roll out the plain butter cookie mixture to a 12in x 4½in rectangle, about ⅝in thick. Keep the dough in a neat block as you work, so that very little of the mixture will need to be trimmed off once the checkerboard pattern is shaped. Repeat with the chocolate butter cookie mixture.

2 Brush the plain dough with a small amount of beaten egg white. This will help the two pastes to adhere

butter cookie mixture (see page 9)
chocolate butter cookie mixture (see page 9)
small amount of beaten egg white
small amount of flour
icing and decoration
2½oz semisweet chocolate
2½oz white chocolate
equipment
large cookie sheet
rolling pin
pastry brush

sharp knife
wire cooling rack
paper piping bags
makes 60
baking time 12–15 minutes

24

together. Carefully lay the chocolate dough over the top of the plain dough.

3 Use a sharp, lightly floured knife to cut the mixture in half, lengthways. Brush one of the halves with egg white and then stack the other half on top, so that the colors alternate. Take care to line up the cut edges of the doughs. Carefully trim off the uncut edges of the dough.

4 Use the lightly floured knife to cut the dough block lengthways into four even-sized strips. Reflour the knife after each cut if the dough begins to stick to the surface of the blade.

5 Reassemble the stack so that the colors alternate, creating a checkerboard design. Do not forget to brush each layer with egg white to secure them together.

6 Slice the stack widthways into ¼in slices and transfer the pieces to the cookie sheet, spacing them slightly apart from each other. Bake for 12–15 minutes until the squares just begin to darken around the edges. Leave the pieces on the cookie sheet for 2 minutes before transferring them to a wire cooling rack.

7 Break the semisweet and white chocolate into pieces in separate bowls, and melt them over a saucepan of hot

water. Put the melted chocolates in paper piping bags and snip off the merest tip of each. Use the plain chocolate to pipe decorative dots and lines on to half the cookies. Use the white chocolate to pipe decorations over the remaining squares.

Leave the squares to set in a cool place for about 2 hours before transferring them to an airtight container.

Shaping these checkerboards is so much easier, and the definition of the pattern will be clearly distinguishable, if the dough is really well chilled. If the mixture starts sticking to the knife, particularly when you come to step 5, put the dough in the freezer for about 10 minutes to firm up. Likewise, if the dough is soft once the cookies have been shaped, pop them in the freezer on the cookie sheets for a little while and they will retain a better shape while baking.

If you prefer a generous amount of chocolate on your cookies, melt some extra chocolate and dip the backs of the squares into the liquid. Allow the excess chocolate to drip back into the pan, before placing the cookies, chocolate-side down, on baking parchment. Alternatively, dip just the sides of the squares in chocolate, and then roll them in chopped hazelnuts.

Chocolate mosaic eggs

Ideal for chocoholics, these eggs use three kinds of chocolate. For presentation, try hanging them from window frames, or put them in a box lined with tissue paper.

1 Preheat the oven to 350°F and grease two large cookie sheets. Put the flour, spice, and butter in a food processor and blend until the mixture resembles fine breadcrumbs. Add the apricots, sugar, and egg, and mix thoroughly to create a dough. (If you do not have a food processor, you can combine the flour and spice in a bowl, and then rub the butter into this mixture by hand. Then mix in the apricots, sugar, and egg.)

2 Turn the dough mixture out on to a lightly floured surface and roll it out to ¼in thickness. Use the cookie

2 cups all-purpose flour
2 teaspoons ground allspice
½ cup unsalted butter
¾ cup dried apricots, roughly chopped
¾ cup light brown sugar
1 egg
icing and decoration
3½oz milk chocolate
3½oz semisweet chocolate
3½oz white chocolate
fine ribbon

equipment
2 large cookie sheets
rolling pin
2½in round cookie cutter
metal skewer
wire cooling rack
paper piping bags
makes 24
baking time 12–15 minutes

cutter to cut out as many round shapes as possible. Odd scraps of dough can be pushed together and rerolled, to ensure that all the mixture gets used – you should be able to make about 24 pieces.

3 To make the circles into egg shapes, place about three pieces in a row and push a rolling pin over them, increasing the pressure as you roll. The circles should become elongated and egg-shaped.

4 Transfer the pieces to the cookie sheets. Use the metal skewer to make holes in the top ends of the shapes about ½in away from the edges. Bake for 12–15 minutes until

golden. Re-mark the holes if the cookies have risen slightly during cooking. Transfer the pieces to a wire rack and leave to cool.

5 Break up the chocolate into separate bowls and melt each over a saucepan of hot water. Put the milk chocolate in a piping bag and snip off the merest tip. Pipe a line on to each egg shape, about ⅛in from the edge. Pipe further random lines inside the piped border, first in one direction and then the other.

6 Put the semisweet chocolate into another piping bag and snip off the tip. Use this to fill in some of the

patterned shapes created by the milk chocolate piping. Aim to fill around half the number of shapes.

Use the metal skewer to ease the melted chocolate into the corners of the piped shapes. (Tapping the cookie gently on the surface sometimes helps to spread the chocolate.) Do not be tempted to overfill the areas – otherwise the chocolate may run over the edges.

Put the white chocolate into another piping bag and use this to fill the remaining sections of the cookies. Again, use the (cleaned) skewer to take the chocolate right up to the edges. Leave to set slightly. Pipe more milk chocolate

over the original lines to accentuate the shapes. Leave the eggs aside to set in a cool place before storing on a tray, covered with plastic wrap for up to two days.

Cut varying lengths of ribbon and thread these through the holes in the cookies so that they can be hung up.

TIP Cut the smallest amount possible off the tip of the milk chocolate piping bag. This is because warm chocolate flows out very quickly, and so you need to be able to control the icing. (You can easily cut off a fraction more if necessary.) The recipe works equally well with the plain or chocolate butter mixture on page 9.

Easter chicks

These cute chicks make bright, fun gifts or ideal table decorations at birthday and christening parties. Tie them in bundles or arrange them in a nest display.

1 Preheat the oven to 400°F and grease two cookie sheets. Trace the two chick templates (see page 124) on to paper and cut them out. Roll out the chosen dough on a floured surface and cut out the chick shapes using the templates and a small, sharp knife or X-acto knife. Transfer the pieces to the cookie sheets.

2 If you are using the butter cookie mixture, bake the chicks for about 8–10 minutes. If you are using the light gingerbread mixture, bake the chicks for about 12 minutes. Leave the chicks to stand on the cookie

butter cookie or light gingerbread mixture (see pages 8 and 9)

icing and decoration

yellow and blue food coloring

icing glaze (see page 9)

royal icing (see page 9)

1oz orange rolled fondant

confectioners' sugar, for dusting

equipment

2 cookie sheets

paper for template (see page 124)

rolling pin

small, sharp knife or X-acto knife

wire cooling rack

pastry brush

paper piping bag

medium writing tip

fine paintbrush

makes about 16

baking time 8–12 minutes

sheets for 2 minutes, before transferring them to a wire rack to cool.

3 Add some yellow food coloring to the icing glaze. Then, using a pastry brush, spread a layer of glaze over all the chicks. Take the glaze right up to the edges to create a thin, even surface.

4 Spoon some royal icing into a piping bag fitted with a medium writing tip. Carefully pipe around the outlines of the wings, then around the edges of the chicks. Next, pipe blobs of icing for the eyes. Leave them to dry for about an hour.

5 Thinly roll the orange fondant over a surface dusted with confectioners' sugar and cut out shapes for the beaks. For the chicks in profile, cut a beak shape using the template as a size guide. For the other chicks, cut out tiny diamond shapes, then pinch them gently to fold the fondant into beak shapes. Secure the beaks to the chicks with a dampened paintbrush. Dilute a small amount of blue food coloring with a little water and use this to paint in the centers of the eyes.

TIP For a special presentation, arrange the chicks in small boxes, baskets, or other containers and surround them with shredded paper and chocolate mini eggs.

Chocolate box

A chocolate lover's heaven! These lavishly coated chocolate goodies are great for serving with coffee, or as a boxed-up gift at any time of year.

Finely chop the butter and put this, along with the flour and cocoa powder, into a food processor. Blend until the mixture resembles fine breadcrumbs. Mix in the sugar, egg yolks, and molasses to form a dough.

Roll the mixture under the palms of your hands into a thick, even sausage, about 12in long and 1½in wide. Neaten the ends of the sausage, then wrap in plastic wrap and chill for at least 30 minutes. Preheat the oven to 400°F and grease a large cookie sheet.

¼ cup butter
1½ cups self-rising flour
¼ cup cocoa powder
⅓ cup light brown sugar
2 egg yolks
⅙ cup molasses
icing and decoration
5oz white chocolate
5oz milk chocolate
5oz semisweet chocolate
10–12 chocolate-coated coffee beans

cocoa powder for dusting
equipment
plastic wrap
large cookie sheet
sharp knife
wire cooling rack
baking parchment
grater
paper piping bags
makes about 30
baking time 10 minutes

3 Use a sharp knife to cut the mixture into ⅜in thick slices and transfer them to the cookie sheet. Bake for 10 minutes until slightly risen, then transfer the pieces to a wire rack to cool.

4 Finely grate ½oz white chocolate. Melt the remaining white chocolate in one bowl, and the milk and semisweet chocolates in two separate bowls. Then line a tray with baking parchment.

5 Dip a third of the cookies in the melted white chocolate, allowing excess chocolate to drip into the bowl. Transfer to the tray and sprinkle with grated white chocolate.

6 Place a spoonful of melted milk and semisweet chocolate into separate piping bags and keep in a warm place. Coat half the cookies in the remaining milk chocolate and half in the semisweet chocolate, using a fork as before, and transfer them to the paper-lined tray.

7 Snip the merest tip off the two piping bags. Scribble freehand lines of milk chocolate over each of the plain chocolate-covered cookies.

8 Pipe swirls of semisweet chocolate over the milk chocolate–covered cookies and decorate with a chocolate coffee bean. Leave the cookies in a cool place to set.

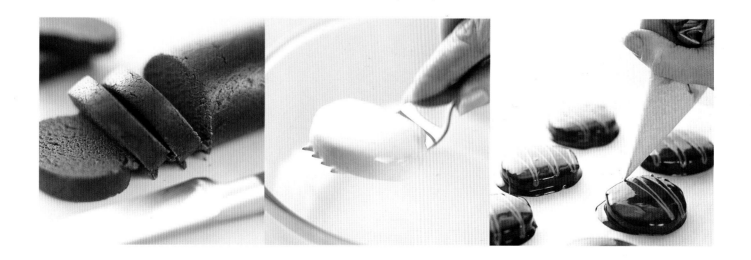

Special occasions

Butterflies

Use contrasting colors, such as those shown here, to decorate these butterflies. Once set, arrange them in a tissue-lined shallow box to make a stunning gift.

1 Preheat the oven to 400°F and grease two cookie sheets. Trace the butterfly templates on page 125 on to paper and cut them out. Roll out the butter cookie mixture on a floured surface and then carefully cut out the butterfly shapes using the templates and a small, sharp knife or X-acto knife.

2 Transfer the shapes to the cookie sheets and reroll the trimmings to make more shapes. Bake the butterflies for about 8 minutes until they turn a pale golden color around the edges. Leave the pieces on the cookie sheets

butter cookie mixture (see page 9)
icing and decoration
double quantity of royal icing (see page 9)
blue or purple and green or lilac food coloring
small white cake-decorating stamens
equipment
2 cookie sheets
paper for template (see page 125)
rolling pin
sharp knife or X-acto knife
wire cooling rack

baking parchment
paper piping bags
fine writing tip
toothpicks
makes 20–24
baking time 8 minutes

for 5 minutes before transferring them to a wire rack so that they can cool.

Fit a paper piping bag with a fine writing tip. Fill the bag with a small amount of the royal icing. Spoon some more royal icing into another piping bag.

Divide the remaining icing between two bowls. Color the icing in one bowl blue or purple, and the icing in the other bowl green or lilac. Thin each quantity of icing with a few drops of water. A flat surface should form when the icing is left to stand for a minute. Transfer the colored icings to separate piping bags.

Using the royal icing in the bag fitted with the writing tip, pipe a line of icing around the edges of the front wings, then around the back wings so that the ends almost meet in the center.

Snip off the tip of the piping bag with the remaining white icing so the icing flows in a thick line. Use this to pipe a coil shape down the centers of the butterflies, allowing the icing to trail off to a point at the end.

Snip off the tip of the piping bag containing the blue or purple icing. Using a scribbling action, flood the wing sections of one butterfly with icing to create a lacy effect.

(If you overfill the sections with icing, it will spread to fill the wings entirely. This also looks effective although you will not achieve the lacy texture.) Ease the icing into the wing tip areas with toothpicks.

Snip off the tip of the piping bag containing the green or lilac icing. Pipe three small dots on to the back wings of the iced cookies.

Pipe three larger dots of icing into the icing on the front wings. Push a toothpick into each dot of icing and gently draw it down the length of the wing to create a feathered finish. Complete about half the number of butterflies in this way, then reverse the colors to decorate the remaining butterfly shapes.

Pipe a large dot of white icing at the front of each body. Cut the stamens down to $\frac{1}{2}$in lengths and press two into each butterfly for antennae. Leave to set until the icing is hard. Store in a large, airtight tin, interleaved with baking parchment.

TIP Remember to complete each butterfly with colored icing before going on to the next shape. This is because the icing forms a crust quite quickly and delays could prevent the colors from feathering together properly.

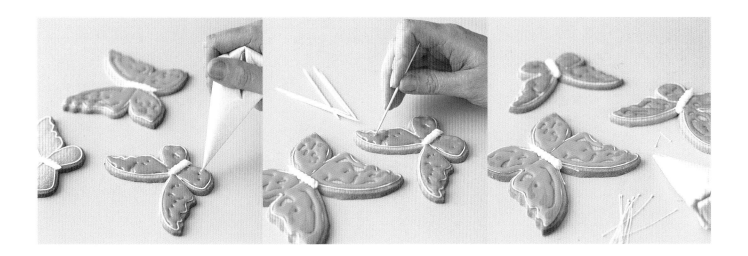

Christening cookies

An assortment of prettily decorated cookies makes an eyecatching spread of pastel colors for a christening celebration or little girl's party.

1 Preheat the oven to 400°F and lightly grease two cookie sheets. Thinly roll out the butter cookie mixture on a floured surface and cut out shapes using the cookie cutters. Reroll the trimmings to make more cookies. (If you do not have many types of cookie cutters, use a knife to cut out 2in squares. Alternatively, make diamond shapes by cutting the dough into thick strips and then cutting diagonal lines across the strips.)

2 Place the shapes on the cookie sheets and bake for around 6–8 minutes, until the pieces turn a pale, golden

butter cookie mixture (see page 9)
icing and decoration
double quantity royal icing (see page 9)
pink, blue, and yellow food coloring
silver dragées
equipment
2 cookie sheets
selection of small cookie cutters, about 2in in diameter (such as heart, petal, diamond, star, circle, and teardrop)
wire cooling rack

paper piping bags
makes 60
baking time 6–8 minutes

color around the edges. Leave to stand for a couple of minutes, before transferring to a wire rack to cool.

3 Divide the royal icing equally into four bowls. Add a little pink coloring to one bowl, blue to the second, and yellow to the third. The remaining portion of royal icing should be left white. Transfer the colored icings to separate piping bags and snip off the tip of each bag so that the icing flows in a fine line.

4 Thin the white icing with a few drops of water to give it a slightly thinner consistency than the colored varieties. Spoon this mixture into another piping bag and snip off a slightly larger tip so that the icing flows in a broader line of about $1/4$in thick.

5 To decorate the stars and diamond-shaped cookies, pipe three alternate lines of blue and yellow icing around the edges of the cookies, leaving a small gap between each line. Fill in the centers of the shapes with dots of icing in both colors.

6 To decorate the heart and petal shapes, pipe large dots of pink or yellow icing around the edges of the cookies. Pipe an additional row of pink or yellow dots inside the first line. Press silver dragées at evenly spaced intervals

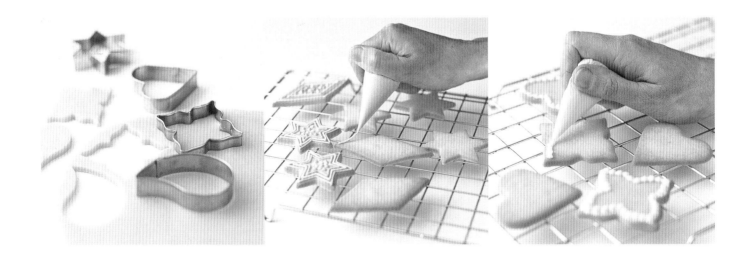

into the icing. Work on a couple of cookies at a time, so that the icing is still soft enough to secure the dragées.

To decorate the round cookies, pipe swirls of the white icing over the top of them. Work from the edges into the center of the cookies, letting the icing flood over the surface a little. Use the same technique for the teardrop shapes, bringing the icing to a point. Pipe casual lines of blue and pink icing over the white, so that the colors run into each other slightly.

Leave the shapes aside for about 2 hours. Once completely set, arrange the pieces in shallow, airtight containers, stacking them no more than two deep. Weave sheets of baking parchment between each layer to help protect the shapes and prevent the icing from melting, or becoming crushed.

TIPS These shapes would also make a good choice for a wedding celebration. Use simple white icing or match the color scheme of the dresses and flowers.

Made using Christmas cookie cutters and vibrant icing colors, the small cookies would also make ideal decorations for the festive season. Use cookie cutters such as holly leaves, stars, and angels for a seasonal feel.

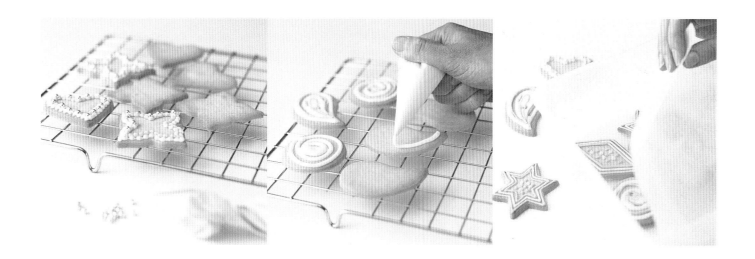

Birthday initials

These little apricot shortbreads can be decorated with the initials of guests at a birthday party, or with a special celebratory message.

1 Preheat the oven to 400°F. Grease the baking pan and line it with baking parchment. Then grease the paper. Reserve a third of the butter cookie mixture, and roll out the remainder into a rectangle about the size of the pan base. Place the mixture in the pan, pressing it around the corners to form an even layer. Prick the base with a fork.

2 Bake for 20 minutes until just beginning to color around the edges. Meanwhile, press the jam through the sieve into a bowl using the back of a spoon. Add a few

butter cookie mixture (see page 9)
icing and decoration
8oz apricot jam
small amount of orange food coloring (optional)
royal icing (see page 9)
silver or gold dragées
equipment
11in x 7in rectangular, shallow baking pan
baking parchment
rolling pin
sieve

small alphabet cookie cutters
sharp knife
paper piping bag
medium writing tip
makes 18
baking time 35 minutes

drops of orange food coloring if you wish. Spread the jam in an even layer over the baked mixture in the pan.

Roll out the remaining dough on a floured surface into one long strip. Cut out two 11in x ½in strips and place them over the jam, against the long sides of the pan. Cut two 7in x ½in strips and position them along the short sides of the pan. Cut two 11in x ¾in strips and arrange them at even spaces down the length of the pan. Finally, cut five 7in x ¾in strips and position them at even intervals across the width of the pan. The aim of this stage is to create a kind of lattice effect across the surface of the base cookies.

Reroll the trimmings and cut out the letters using the alphabet cookie cutters or a knife. Arrange these in the individual squares. Bake for a further 15 minutes or until just beginning to color. Leave to cool in the pan.

Lift the cookie out of the pan and peel away the lining paper. Trim off the edges of the cookie, then cut through the strips carefully to make individual squares.

Put some royal icing in a piping bag and pipe lines around the edges of each square, pressing a dragée into each corner as you work. Pipe further lines over the letters. Leave aside to set and store for up to four days.

Decorated with almonds and exotic dried fruits, shortbreads can be enjoyed on any occasion. Bunched into parcels with ribbon, they make stylish decorations.

Preheat the oven to 325°F. Grease the baking pan, line it with the baking parchment, and then grease the paper. Cut the butter into small pieces and put this, along with the flour, into a food processor. Keep the machine turned on until the mixture resembles fine breadcrumbs. Add the sugar and blend until the mixture forms a paste. (Alternatively, put the flour in a bowl and add the finely chopped butter. Rub the butter into the flour with your fingertips, until the mixture begins to bind together. Then add the sugar and mix to the paste in the same way.)

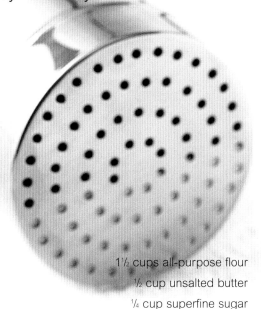

1½ cups all-purpose flour
½ cup unsalted butter
¼ cup superfine sugar
icing and decoration
1 cup mixed dried fruits (such as mango or papaya)
¼ cup slivered almonds
¾ cup confectioners' sugar
4–5 teaspoons rosewater
length of wired ribbon

equipment
11in x 7in rectangular, shallow baking pan
baking parchment
large, sharp knife
wire cooling rack
makes 10 parcels
baking time 35 minutes

Pack the paste into the tin and press it down with your fingertips, to create a level surface. Prick the base with a fork and bake the mixture for about 35 minutes, until it turns a slight golden color around the edges.

Meanwhile, cut the dried pieces of fruit into very small pieces. Lightly toast the almonds. Add the confectioners' sugar to the rosewater and beat the mixture together until it forms the consistency of a thin, pouring cream.

While still warm, make deep cuts into the mixture with a knife. The idea is to create small 'fingers,' each

measuring about 3½ x ⅝in. Leave aside to cool down for about 10 minutes.

Spread the icing over the baked mixture, until it is covered with a thin, even layer. Make sure that you can still see the cut lines through the icing. (You may not need to use all of the icing.)

Decorate each shortbread finger with a row of dried fruits and nuts, then leave them to cool completely.

Using a large, sharp knife, trace the cut marks and separate into fingers. Tie into bundles with the ribbon.

Seashore shapes

Making two or three different cookies with the same theme allows the designs to complement each other. These seaside shapes are ideal for summer occasions.

1 Preheat the oven to 400°F. Grease two cookie sheets. Trace the shell and starfish templates on page 124 on to paper and cut them out. Roll out the gingerbread mixture on a floured surface and cut out the shell and starfish shapes using the templates and a small, sharp knife or X-acto knife. (Make about the same amount of each shape.) Transfer the shapes to the prepared cookie sheets and reroll the trimmings to make more shapes.

2 Bake for about 12 minutes until the shapes begin to darken around the edges. Leave them on the cookie

light gingerbread mixture (see page 8)
icing and decoration
¾ cup unsalted butter, softened
3 cups confectioners' sugar, sifted
1 tablespoon cocoa powder, sifted
pink food coloring
equipment
2 cookie sheets
paper for template (see page 124)
rolling pin
small, sharp knife or X-acto knife

wire cooling rack
paper piping bags
makes 34–38
baking time 12 minutes

sheets for about 2 minutes to harden, before transferring them to a wire rack to cool.

3 To make the buttercream, beat the butter in a bowl until soft and creamy. Gradually beat in the confectioners' sugar until the mixture is smooth and pale. (If the mixture remains firm, add a few drops of boiling water to soften it.) Transfer a large spoonful of the buttercream to a separate bowl and beat in the cocoa powder to make chocolate buttercream. Place in a paper piping bag and snip off the tip. Transfer about a third of the remaining buttercream to a separate bowl and beat in a little pink food coloring. Transfer to another piping bag and snip off

the tip. Place some of the plain buttercream in a third piping bag and snip off the tip.

4 Pipe a line of buttercream around the edges of the starfish, about 1/8in away from the edges. Pipe two or three more lines just inside the first. (Do not worry about making the piping too perfect on the cookies. The "casual" look of the piping is effective on these shapes and is particularly appropriate to buttercream.)

5 On the scallop shapes, fill in the square ends with buttercream, then pipe looped lines of buttercream up to the scalloped edges and back to the base.

On the periwinkle shapes, pipe semicircles of icing on to each section of the shells, starting at the pointed end. Fill in the cookies with lines of piping, running lengthways across the surface.

Fill in the centers of the starfish cookies with several lines of pink buttercream. Decorate the centers of the starfish with dots of the chocolate buttercream.

Use the chocolate and pink buttercream to pipe decorative details on to the other shapes. Store the cookies in a single layer in a cool place for up to two days until ready to serve.

Young children tend to love these kinds of shapes, although you may prefer to use brighter colors as decoration for birthday parties.

Do not stack the shapes during storage as buttercream never sets hard and the icing may become damaged.

This recipe produces a large quantity of cookie mixture, so you may prefer to use only half the amount and freeze the remaining dough for a later date. Alternatively, you could simply make plain gingerbread cookies – the buttercream quantity can easily be halved, to ensure there is no wastage.

The piped decoration on these stylish tuiles is completed before they are even baked, so all you have to do is shape them once they come out of the oven.

Preheat the oven to 375°F. Line two cookie sheets with nonstick paper and lightly grease the paper. Then, melt the butter.

Whisk the egg whites in a bowl with the sugar until smooth. Whisk in the flour, cream, and melted butter to make a loose paste. Spoon 3 tablespoons of the mixture into a small bowl and beat in the cocoa powder until smooth. Transfer the cocoa paste to the piping bag and snip off the tip so that the paste flows out in a line about 1/8in thick.

2 tablespoons unsalted butter

3 egg whites

1/2 cup superfine sugar

5 tablespoons all-purpose flour

2 tablespoons heavy cream

2 teaspoons cocoa powder, sifted

equipment

2 cookie sheets

nonstick paper

paper piping bag

rolling pin

wire cooling rack

makes 20

baking time 8 minutes

Place 6 scant tablespoons of the paste on to one cookie sheet. Spread each to about 2¾in in diameter, and allow plenty of space between each.

Pipe a small amount of the chocolate paste into each circle of mixture. You can make a variety of patterns, including wavy lines, coils, or dots. However, do keep the piping about ½in away from the edge of each piece, to prevent it from bleeding away.

Bake in the oven for about 8 minutes until the edges are golden. (Prepare a second batch of tuiles while the first is baking.)

Once baked, peel the paper off the tuiles and lay them over a rolling pin so that they set with a curved shape. When the second batch is baked, the first can be transferred from the rolling pin to a wire rack.

TIPS If the baked cookies turn crisp before you have managed to shape them around the rolling pin, pop them back in the oven for a few moments. This will help to soften them.

For extra decoration, roll the edges in 3oz semisweet melted chocolate. Then place them on a sheet of baking parchment to set.

Small, rectangular butter cookies make excellent place cards for wedding tables. If you have a color scheme, you can always add highlights to the icing.

Preheat the oven to 400°F. Grease two cookie sheets. Thinly roll out the mixture on a floured surface and cut out 3in x 2in rectangles, rerolling the trimmings to make extra pieces. Transfer the shapes to the cookie sheets and bake for about 8–10 minutes, until they turn a pale, golden color around the edges. Allow to stand for a couple of minutes before moving to a wire cooling rack.

Put some royal icing in a piping bag fitted with a fine writing tip. Pipe names across the cookies, keeping

butter cookie mixture (see page 9)
icing and decoration
double quantity royal icing (see page 9)
edible silver or colored metallic dusting powder, also called petal dust or blossom tint
equipment
2 cookie sheets
rolling pin
sharp knife
wire cooling rack
paper piping bag
fine writing tip
baking parchment (optional)
fine sieve
makes 28
baking time 8–10 minutes

61

the letters away from the edges. (You may prefer to practice writing a few names on a sheet of baking parchment first.)

Pipe a line of icing around the edges of the name to create an oval-shaped frame. Pipe loops of icing that just meet the first line and form points around the edges of the rectangles.

Use more icing to fill in the centers of the loops, generously filling each section. Pipe further curved lines in the gaps around the edges. Leave the place names to set for at least 2 hours.

Put a little dusting powder/petal dust/blossom tint in a fine sieve. Holding it about 4in above the cookies, lightly sprinkle the dusting powder over the place cards. Transfer the shapes to an airtight container and store in a cool place for up to three days.

Once the cookies are set, they can be stacked in an airtight container. However, do not make the piles any deeper than three cookies, and weave baking parchment between each layer. If you have time, it is better to dust the cookies (step 5) on the actual day of the celebration. The place cards can also be used for other occasions, such as special dinner parties.

Toucans

These cheerful birds will certainly add color and fun to a special family tea or celebration. Perch them among plant foliage for extra effect.

Preheat the oven to 400°F. Grease two cookie sheets. Trace the toucan template on page 124 on to paper and cut it out. Roll out the mixture on a floured surface and cut out the toucan shapes using the template and a sharp knife.

Transfer the toucan shapes to the cookie sheets and bake them in the oven for about 12 minutes, until they turn a deep golden color. Leave the birds on the cookie sheets for a couple of minutes, before carefully transferring them to a wire rack to cool.

light gingerbread mixture (see page 8)

icing and decoration

royal icing (see page 9)

blue food coloring

3oz red rolled fondant

confectioners' sugar for dusting

2oz white rolled fondant

1oz orange rolled fondant

equipment

2 cookie sheets

paper for template (see page 124)

rolling pin

sharp knife

wire cooling rack

paper piping bags

fine writing tip

toothpicks

fine paintbrush

makes 12–14

baking time 12 minutes

3 Add blue food coloring to the royal icing and transfer about a third of the quantity to a piping bag fitted with a fine writing tip. Thin the remaining blue icing until it has the consistency of thick pouring cream and transfer the mixture into another piping bag.

4 Thinly roll the red fondant on a surface dusted with confectioners' sugar. Use the template to cut out beaks and position these on the birds, securing the fondant into position with a small amount of the unthinned royal icing. With the tip of the knife, define the upper and lower areas of the beak by marking a slightly curved line across the surface of the fondant.

5 Using the unthinned icing, pipe a line from the top of the beak along the outline of the bird. Take the icing up and around the edge of the wing but leave space for the white breast to be positioned. Pipe another line around the edge of the breast to the bottom of the beak. Repeat on all the toucans.

6 Snip off the tip of the thinned icing bag and use this to flood the icing over the toucans, within the piped lines. The icing should fill the area in a thin, even layer. Use a wooden toothpick to spread the icing to the edges and corners. Leave the birds aside to set for about an hour.

Thinly roll the white fondant and cut out the breasts using the template and knife. Position the breastplates on the birds, securing them with a small amount of royal icing from the bag. Press firmly, to ensure the rolled fondant adheres to the surface.

Roll out the orange fondant into a thin layer and cut out the eyes. Press these gently into position on the blue icing, again using some royal icing to hold the rolled fondant in position.

Using blue food coloring and a fine paintbrush, paint on the eyes and feather details. Leave the birds aside to set

overnight. You can store the cookies in an airtight container for up to three days.

TIPS Once you have used the toucan templates to cut out the cookie shapes, cut out the beak, breastplate, and eye shapes from the template. The small paper pieces can then be used to cut out the rolled fondant shapes more accurately.

Try alternative color combinations to imitate the colorful plumage of tropical birds. Combinations of bright orange, yellow, blue, green, and red are all extremely effective, and will brighten any table arrangement or room.

Giant birthday cookie

Presenting one huge cookie makes the perfect gift for anyone who prefers eating cookies to cakes! Arrange it in a shallow box with candles for extra effect.

1 cup self-rising flour

1⅓ cups porridge oats

½ teaspoon baking soda

½ cup unsalted butter

generous ½ cup light brown sugar

3 tablespoons corn syrup

icing and decoration

¾ cup confectioners' sugar

4–5 teaspoons lemon juice

1½ cups mixed dried fruits (such as mango, papaya, and melon)

1 Preheat the oven to 350°F. Place the flan ring or loose-base cake pan on a cookie sheet and lightly grease. Alternatively, grease the cake pan. Mix together the flour, oats, and soda. Melt the butter in a saucepan with the light brown sugar and corn syrup. Pour over the flour mixture and mix until evenly combined. Transfer to the flan ring or loose-base cake pan and spread almost to the edges.

2 Bake for 15–18 minutes until golden. (The mixture will be very soft and wobbly but will firm up on cooling.)

⅓ cup unblanched almonds, roughly halved

equipment

9in plain flan ring or loose-base cake pan

cookie sheet

wire cooling rack

paper piping bag

makes 1

baking time 15–18 minutes

Loosen the mixture from the edges of the pan and leave for 10 minutes, then transfer to a wire rack to cool.

3 To make the icing, blend the confectioners' sugar with the lemon juice until the mixture thickly coats the back of a spoon. Spoon into a piping bag and snip off the tip so the icing flows in a line about ¼in thick.

4 Pipe a wavy line of icing around the edges of the cookie to within ½in of the edges.

5 Mix together the dried fruits and nuts and arrange them over the icing, pressing them down gently.

6 Using more icing from the bag, scribble lines back and forth over the fruit and nuts as decoration. Pipe the recipient's name, or a birthday message, into the center of the cookie. Leave to set for a couple of hours before packaging or storing. Keep in an airtight container for up to three days.

TIP If you are nervous about piping the name or message on to the cookie, cut out small letters in thin card and lay them on the center of the surface. Transfer the icing to another paper piping bag and snip off a much smaller tip. Pipe around the letters, then remove them and fill in the centers with more icing.

Ladybugs

Add a splash of color to a party with a family of ladybugs. If you do not have small, round cookie cutters to shape the spots, use the ends of piping tips.

1 Preheat the oven to 400°F. Grease two cookie sheets. Trace the ladybug body and head templates on page 124 on to paper and cut out.

2 Roll out the butter cookie mixture on a floured surface and cut out the body shapes using the template and a small, sharp knife or X-acto knife. (Keep the template for shaping the red icing.) Reroll the trimmings and cut out an equal number of heads. Transfer the pieces to the cookie sheets. Bake for about 8–10 minutes until they turn golden around the edges. Transfer to a wire cooling rack.

butter cookie mixture (see page 9)

icing and decoration

royal icing (see page 9)

7oz red rolled fondant

confectioners' sugar for dusting

3oz black rolled fondant

equipment

2 cookie sheets

paper for templates (see page 124)

rolling pin

small, sharp knife or X-acto knife

wire cooling rack

paper piping bag

medium writing tip

1in and ⅝in round cookie cutters

paintbrush

makes 12

baking time 8–10 minutes

3 Put some royal icing into a paper piping bag fitted with a medium writing tip. Thinly roll the red fondant on a surface lightly dusted with confectioners' sugar. Use the knife and template to cut out the bodies of the ladybugs.

4 Pipe a small amount of icing on to the ladybug shapes and position the red rolled fondant on top. Secure the heads in place with a little more icing.

5 Roll out the black fondant very thinly and cut out plenty of circles using the two small, round cookie cutters. Secure in position using a dampened paintbrush. For the

dots right on the edges of the ladybugs, simply position them so they overhang, then cut off the excess paste with a small, sharp knife or X-acto knife.

6 Using the icing in the bag, pipe large blobs for the eyes and then the antennae. Roll small balls of black fondant and press them into the centers of the eyes, for the pupils. Roll some larger balls for the ends of the antennae and fix into position. Shape and secure each mouth using red icing trimmings.

7 Leave the ladybugs aside for 2 hours before storing them in an airtight container for up to three days.

Juggling clowns

These wacky colors and fun features make clowns the perfect characters for children's parties. Prop them up against tumblers and dishes for instant color.

1 Preheat the oven to 400°F and grease two cookie sheets. Trace the template on page 124 on to paper and cut it out.

2 Roll out the light gingerbread mixture on a floured surface and cut out the clown shapes using the template. Transfer the pieces to the cookie sheets and bake them for 12–15 minutes until they turn a golden color around the edges. Leave the pieces on the tray for around 2 minutes to harden slightly, before transferring them to a wire cooling rack.

light gingerbread mixture (see page 8)

icing and decoration

royal icing (see page 9)

confectioners' sugar for dusting

4oz blue rolled fondant

4oz lilac rolled fondant

3oz orange rolled fondant

2oz red rolled fondant

equipment

2 cookie sheets

paper for template (see page 124)

rolling pin

sharp knife

wire cooling rack

paper piping bags

fine and large writing tips

fine paintbrush

baking parchment

makes 16

baking time 12–15 minutes

3 Put some royal icing in a piping bag fitted with a fine writing tip. Spoon more of the icing into a piping bag fitted with a large writing tip.

4 Lightly dust the work surface with confectioners' sugar. Roll the blue and lilac fondant under the palms of your hands into two thin sausages. Press the two pieces together and then fold, twist, and roll them into each other about three times, so that the colors become lightly marbled.

5 Roll the marbled fondant into a thin layer. Remove the hands, feet, and head from the clown template, to leave just the suit, and use this to cut out a suit shape in the icing. Pipe a small amount of icing on to a cookie and secure the fondant suit in position, smoothing it down gently with your fingers. Repeat this process with the remaining shapes. You may need to reroll the trimmings in order to get extra suits – this will probably cause the colors to become even more marbled.

6 Thinly roll the orange fondant and use a knife to cut out shapes for the hats and boots. (You can use the template as a guide if necessary.) Secure these pieces of fondant to the clowns using a small amount of royal icing, as before. Shape small buttons out of the

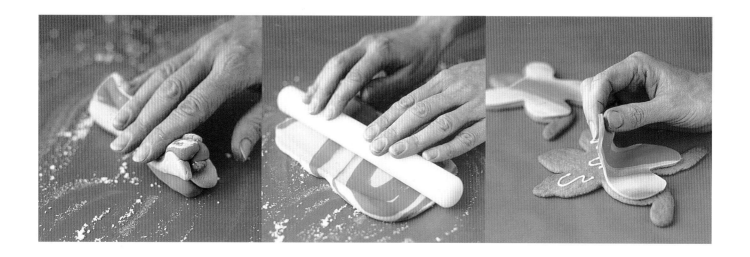

fondant and carefully secure these to the clowns' suits with a dampened paintbrush.

7 Roll out the red fondant thinly and cut out shapes for the pockets. Use the dampened paintbrush and icing to secure these to the suits. Roll tiny balls of icing for the noses and curved shapes for the mouths. Secure the pieces with dots of icing from the bag with the fine writing tip. Roll small balls of the blue icing trimmings and secure these at the tops of the hats.

8 Use the piping bag fitted with the large writing tip to pipe the frilly collars. Use the icing bag with the fine tip to add the wrists and ankles. Finish by piping on the eye and mouth details. Leave the clowns aside to set for 2 hours.

9 Store the clowns for up to four days in an airtight container. Be sure to use a shallow container and interleave baking parchment between each of the cookie layers.

TIP In addition to propping the clowns up on the dining table, they can also be used for decorating the party room. Simply tie fine ribbon around their waists and hang them around the room.

Gingerbread spice hearts

These aromatic, spice-studded hearts are particularly easy to make and are ideal for anniversaries, Valentine's Day events or rustic, country-style weddings.

1 Preheat the oven to 400°F. Grease two cookie sheets. Roll out the dark gingerbread mixture on a floured surface and cut out heart shapes using the large heart-shaped cookie cutter.

2 Using the smaller cookie cutter, cut out the centers from about half the total number of hearts. Press the whole star anise into the center of the remaining shapes.

3 Transfer all the shapes, including the centers, to the cookie sheets. Bake the shapes for about 12 minutes until

dark gingerbread mixture (see page 8)
about 10 whole star anise
icing and decoration
3 tablespoons cardamom pods
3oz crystallized ginger pieces
1 tablespoon lightly beaten egg white
finely grated rind of half an orange
1 tablespoon orange juice
1¼ cups confectioners' sugar, sifted
3 tablespoons whole cloves

equipment
2 cookie sheets
rolling pin
3in and 1in heart-shaped cookie cutters
wire cooling rack
pestle and mortar
paper piping bag
makes 20
baking time 12 minutes

they have risen slightly. Leave the hearts to stand for a couple of minutes, before transferring them to a wire cooling rack.

4 Using either a pestle and mortar or a small bowl and the end of a rolling pin, lightly crush the cardamom pods to reveal the seeds, then chop the crystallized ginger into very fine pieces.

5 Beat the egg white in a bowl with the orange rind, juice, and confectioners' sugar until the mixture is thick enough to just hold its shape. Spoon this into a piping bag and snip off the tip so that the icing flows in a line about

1/4in thick. Use the icing to pipe thick, wavy lines around the edges of the hearts.

6 Press the cardamom pods, ginger, and cloves into the icing. Leave the hearts aside for 2 hours to set before storing them in an airtight container for up to five days.

TIP If you want to hang the hearts, make a hole 1/2in away from the top of each with a skewer before baking. (Do not forget to reshape the holes when the pieces come out of the oven.) Once decorated, thread with fine ribbon – the hearts can be hung around the room for maximum effect.

Autumn leaves

Capture the stunning colors of fallen, autumnal leaves on these eyecatching treats. It is worth spending some time getting a realistic blend of colors.

1 Preheat the oven to 400°F and grease two cookie sheets. Trace the autumn leaf templates on page 124 on to a sheet of paper and cut out. Roll out the chocolate butter cookie mixture on a floured surface and cut out the leaf shapes, using the templates and a small, sharp knife or an X-acto knife. Make about the same number of leaves in each shape.

2 Transfer the pieces to the cookie sheets and bake for about 12 minutes, until the mixture rises slightly. After baking, transfer the leaf shapes to a wire cooling rack.

chocolate butter cookie mixture (see page 9)

icing and decoration
icing glaze (see page 9)
orange, yellow, and brown food coloring
royal icing (see page 9)

equipment
2 cookie sheets
paper for template (see page 124)
rolling pin
small, sharp knife or X-acto knife
wire cooling rack
paper piping bags
large pastry brush
makes 20
baking time 12 minutes

3 Divide the icing glaze evenly among three small cups or bowls. Color one quantity of the glaze orange, another deep yellow and the third a warm brown. Mix a tablespoonful of each with a third of the royal icing to produce a paler shade of each color. Put these lighter colored icings in piping bags and keep aside for use later.

4 Using the large pastry brush, spread one of the icing glaze colors over one of the leaf shapes, to form a thin covering. Repeat for the other similarly shaped leaves. Then do the same using the other two icing glazes on the remaining two leaf shapes.

5 Pipe fine veins on to each of the leaves, with the piping bags and colored glazes. Use the light orange icing on the orange leaves, the light yellow on the yellow leaves, and so on.

6 Leave the pieces aside to set for about 2–3 hours. They can then be stored in an airtight container for up to four days.

TIP Red and yellow food coloring can be mixed together to make orange, but avoid colors that are too bright and garish. Add a little extra brown to tone colors down, or a little red to warm them up.

Halloween tealights

If you are planning a Halloween night buffet or dinner, these decorative lights will certainly add a sense of atmosphere to the proceedings.

1 Preheat the oven to 400°F. Grease a large cookie sheet. Trace the pumpkin template on page 124 on to a piece of paper and cut it out.

2 Roll out the dark gingerbread mixture on a floured surface and cut around the outer edges of the template with a small, sharp knife. Transfer the pumpkin shape to the cookie sheet. Cut out three more pumpkin shapes, making sure you cut a straight line across the base of each so that they will sit squarely on the bases. Gather up and reroll the trimmings. Use the round cookie cutter

dark gingerbread mixture (see page 8)

icing and decoration

royal icing (see page 9)

orange food coloring

1oz green rolled fondant

confectioners' sugar for dusting

equipment

large cookie sheet

paper for template (see page 124)

rolling pin

small, sharp knife or X-acto knife

2³⁄₄in round cookie cutter

wire cooling rack

paper piping bag

large writing tip

tealights

makes 4

baking time 15 minutes

to cut out four circles for the cookie bases from this remaining gingerbread mixture.

3 Lay the pumpkin template back over the shapes. Cut out and remove the marked features using the tip of a small, sharp knife or an X-acto knife. Bake all the shapes for about 15 minutes until slightly risen. Transfer to a wire cooling rack and leave to cool.

4 Color the royal icing with orange food coloring. Put the icing in a piping bag fitted with a large writing tip. This icing will be used for decorating, and for fixing the rolled fondant.

5 Thinly roll the green fondant on a surface dusted with confectioners' sugar and cut out some small stalk shapes. (Cut out and use the stalk area of the template as a guide if you prefer.) Pipe a little icing on to the stalk area of the pumpkins and position the stalks, gently pressing down the rolled fondant with your fingers. Mark decorative lines on the stalks with the tip of the small, sharp knife or X-acto knife.

6 Use the icing in the bag to pipe an outline around the edges of each pumpkin. Next, outline the holes cut out for the eyes, nose, and mouth. Try to keep a steady hand as you work around the outlines.

7 Pipe more lines from the top of the pumpkins down to the base. Curve piped lines toward the outside edges, to accentuate the round shape of the pumpkins.

8 Pipe several thick, straight lines of icing over the round gingerbread bases, about ½in away from the edges. Gently press the pumpkin pieces into the icing. Pipe another line of icing along the back of the pumpkin where it joins the base – this will help to provide additional support. Prop the pumpkins up with tumblers or small glasses until the icing has set. Leave aside for at least 2 hours, or preferably overnight, to set completely, before storing in an airtight container or tin.

TIPS The pumpkins make attractive decorations for dining tables, shelves, or mantlepieces. Positioning small tealights around the base will help to set them off, and adds to the Halloween atmosphere, although beware that the heat will eventually soften the icing. For a more traditional occasion or children's party, you could always change the facial expressions and replace the smiling mouth with sharp, irregular teeth!

If you do not have any suitable containers that are large enough to store the pumpkin shapes, put them on a tray or board and cover them loosely with plastic wrap. This will help to create an airtight seal.

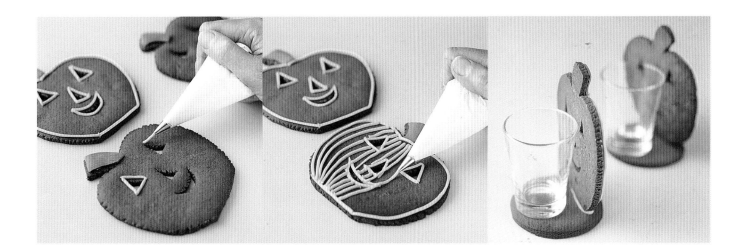

Christmas

Gingerbread cottage

Often associated with the characters Hansel and Gretel, this gingerbread house makes a good cake alternative for a winter birthday or Christmas party.

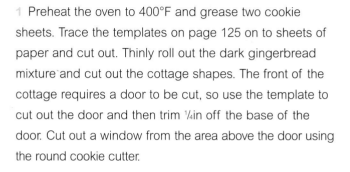

1 Preheat the oven to 400°F and grease two cookie sheets. Trace the templates on page 125 on to sheets of paper and cut out. Thinly roll out the dark gingerbread mixture and cut out the cottage shapes. The front of the cottage requires a door to be cut, so use the template to cut out the door and then trim ¼in off the base of the door. Cut out a window from the area above the door using the round cookie cutter.

2 Transfer all the pieces to the cookie sheets, including the door, and bake for about 15 minutes until slightly risen.

dark gingerbread mixture (see page 8)

icing and decoration

royal icing (see page 9)

10 small ratafia cookies

3oz chocolate-covered raisins

about 15–18 chocolates or small truffles

small packet candy-covered chocolates

7 small wafer-thin chocolate cookies

1 small chocolate-covered fudge bar, thinly sliced

equipment

2 cookie sheets

paper for templates (see page 125)

rolling pin and sharp knife

1½in round cookie cutter

wire cooling rack

paper piping bag

board or rectangular plate, about 11in x 8in

metal spatula

makes 1 cottage

baking time 15 minutes

Leave the pieces on the tray for 2 minutes, before transferring them to a wire cooling rack.

3 Spread a little icing along the base and up the sides of one side section. Spread more icing along the base of the front section and secure the two sections together on the board, propping up the cookies with small glasses or tumblers for support until they have set. Secure the back section, then the other side, and leave for about 30 minutes to set slightly.

4 Spread more icing over the top edges of the side pieces and secure one of the roof sections, again using

glasses or tumblers to give the shapes support. Spread a little icing along the top of the roof and secure the other piece of the roof in place.

5 Using a metal spatula, spread a thin layer of icing over the roof. If the icing feels stiff and will not spread easily, thin it with a little water.

6 For the icicles, hold a teaspoon of icing at an angle above the edges of the roof. As the icing starts to slip from the spoon, catch it along the edges, to create the impression of dangling icicles. (Again, if the icing is too stiff, thin it with a little water first.)

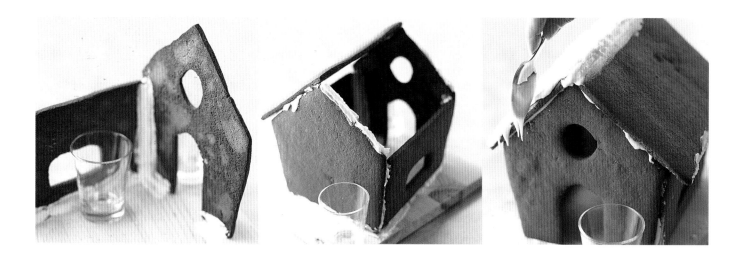

7 Use the ratafia cookies, chocolates, and chocolate-covered raisins to decorate the roof. The pieces can be positioned randomly, but add a single row of chocolate raisins along the top of the roof for the top tiles.

8 Spoon a little more icing into the piping bag and put this aside for later use. Then, spread the remaining icing over the board.

9 Pipe a little icing on to the backs of the chocolate cookies and secure them on either side of the window. Arrange the remaining cookies at the front of the cottage, to create the impression of doorsteps.

10 Pipe a line of icing around the door arch and press the door in position. Decorate the window ledges and round window with chocolate-covered raisins, securing each into position with a dab of icing. Secure another raisin for the doorknob and place a few candy covered disks on the iced-board to suggest a path.

11 Use the icing in the bag to pipe decorative edges around the door and along the corners of the cottage. Add small chocolate fudge slices around the base.

TIP Before positioning the roof, you could fill the house with chocolate and sweet treats for an extra surprise.

Stained-glass candles

In this recipe, crushed fruit candies are baked in gingerbread frames. The idea is that they melt and then set brittle as they cool, to create glasslike panels.

1 Preheat the oven to 400°F. Line two cookie sheets with nonstick paper. Thinly roll out the dark gingerbread mixture on a floured surface and cut out twelve 4³/₄in x 3in rectangles. (You will probably need to cut out the squares from some of the cookies and then reroll the trimmings to make sufficient quantities.) Transfer the rectangles to the lined cookie sheets, spacing them slightly apart so that they do not merge in the oven.

2 Use a square cookie cutter to cut out six squares from each piece, leaving a fine windowpane-effect frame.

dark gingerbread mixture (see page 8)

icing and decoration

8oz hard fruit candies, in a mixture of colors

royal icing (see page 9)

red or orange food coloring

4 nightlights

equipment

2 cookie sheets

nonstick paper

1¹/₄in square cookie cutter or small, sharp knife

rolling pin

toothpicks

paper piping bag

medium writing tip

makes 4 lights

baking time 10 minutes

94

Alternatively, you could use the tip of a knife to cut out the squares. Any of the internal squares that you haven't needed to reroll can be baked separately to avoid wastage. Bake the pieces for 5 minutes, then remove the cookie sheets from the oven and leave aside to cool.

3 Very lightly crush the candies, while still in their wrappers, by tapping them with a rolling pin. (If the candies are not individually wrapped, put them in a plastic bag before crushing them.) Unseal the wrappers/bag and place a few pieces of crushed candy in each square of the frames. (You will need about three candies to fill each rectangle.)

4 Return the cookie sheet to the oven for a further 5 minutes until the candies have melted. If there are any squares that are not completely flooded with the melted candy, use wooden toothpicks to ease the mixture up to the edges. (You will need to do this as soon as the cookies are removed from the oven, because the candy will harden and become brittle very quickly.) Leave the pieces on the cookie sheets to cool completely.

5 Brightly color the royal icing with red or orange food coloring and spoon it into a piping bag fitted with a medium writing tip. Pipe decorative lines over the gingerbread. Leave this to set for about 30 minutes.

6 Carefully peel the paper away from the panels. Pipe a little icing down the edges of three of the cookies and secure them together in a triangle. If necessary, use a few small glasses to prop up the frames until they are set. Repeat with the remaining cookies and leave for about 2 hours or overnight to set.

7 To display, light each nightlight and then lower the frame over the light. The decorations should last at least a full evening without melting – possibly even two or three!

TIPS When removing the cookies from the paper-lined sheets, carefully peel the paper away from the shapes.

This is better than lifting the cookies away from the paper, as the cookie pieces are liable to crack.

Once exposed to the atmosphere, the melted candies will gradually begin to soften, so if you want to make them in advance, leave them on their cookie sheets and cover tightly with plastic wrap for up to three days. For convenience, you can assemble them up to 24 hours before they are required.

To protect the dining table from melted wax, cut triangles of thick card to fit to the base of the nightlights. You can then place them under the decorations and candles.

Lace snowflakes

You will be tempted to keep these stars, with their attractive piped snowflake centers, hanging on the Christmas tree throughout the festive season.

1 Preheat the oven to 400ºF. Lightly grease two cookie sheets. Roll out the butter cookie mixture on a floured surface and cut out star shapes using the large star cookie cutter. Transfer the star shapes to the cookie sheets.

2 Using the small star cookie cutter, cut out the center of each star. If the cookie cutter starts to stick to the dough, clean it and dust with a little flour. Reroll the trimmings as necessary to make 14 star cookies in total. Bake for 6–7 minutes until they turn golden around the edges. Leave

butter cookie mixture (see page 9)
icing and decoration
icing glaze (see page 9)
edible white glitter
royal icing (see page 9)
fine white or silver ribbon
equipment
2 cookie sheets
4½in and 2½in large and small
6-point star cookie cutters
wire cooling rack

baking parchment
pastry brush
fine paintbrush
nonstick paper
paper piping bag
medium writing tip
makes 14
baking time 7 minutes

the cookies on the cookie sheet for 2 minutes, then carefully transfer them to a wire cooling rack.

3 Place a tray or sheet of baking parchment under the rack. (Use two racks or ice cookies in two batches as they will not all fit on one rack.) Using a pastry brush, coat the top side of the stars with icing glaze. Brush any icing away from the inner points with a fine paintbrush. Leave for about 1 hour until touch dry.

4 Brush the stars very lightly with a clean, dampened pastry brush and sprinkle with edible glitter. Do not make the cookies wet because the icing may dissolve.

5 Lift the cookies off the rack and lay them on a sheet of nonstick paper. Shave off any drips of icing from the undersides of the stars if they are not sitting flat on the paper. Put some royal icing in a piping bag fitted with a medium writing tip.

6 Pipe three lines across each star from the inner points of the star so that they cross in the center. Pipe little snowflake designs over the crossed lines as decoration. Leave overnight to set.

7 Carefully peel the paper away and use lengths of ribbon to hang the snowflakes from the tree.

Gift tag trees

These Christmas tree–shaped gift tags really add a personal touch to presents. Thread them with ribbon or string to match the wrapping paper.

1 Preheat the oven to 400°F. Trace the tree template on page 126 on to a sheet of paper and cut out. Grease two cookie sheets.

2 Roll out the butter cookie mixture on a floured surface. Use the template and knife to cut out the tree shapes. Reroll the trimmings if necessary to make 14–16 tree shapes. Transfer to the cookie sheets.

3 Using a skewer, make a small hole near the top of each tree, about ½in away from the edges, ready for

butter cookie mixture (see page 9)
1 cup slivered almonds
icing and decoration
royal icing (see page 9)
dragées
equipment
paper for template (see page 126)
2 cookie sheets
rolling pin
sharp knife
metal skewer

wire cooling rack
paper piping bag
medium writing tip
fine ribbon or string
makes 14–16
baking time 8 minutes

threading the ribbon or string. Make sure each hole measures at least ¹⁄₁₆in across or you may have difficulty threading the ribbon through them.

4 Pick out the perfectly shaped slivered almonds and lightly toast them under a broiler. To decorate the gift tags, arrange the almonds in rows across the dough and press the tops in slightly.

5 Bake for about 8 minutes until golden around the edges. Immediately re-mark the holes as they may have shrunk during baking. Leave on the cookie sheets for 2 minutes, then transfer to a wire cooling rack.

6 Put the icing in a piping bag fitted with a medium writing tip. Pipe wavy lines over the almonds on the cookies. Press dragées into the icing at intervals. Leave to set for about an hour, then transfer to an airtight container.

7 Thread the gift tags with ribbon or string and secure to the wrapped presents.

TIPS To avoid breakages, secure the gift tags to fairly large parcels, and ensure they are well supported.

You will not need all the slivered almonds – this quantity enables you to pick out the best shapes to use.

Christmas baubles

For a really effective Christmas display, thread these baubles on long ribbons and hang them over the mantlepiece or on the Christmas tree.

1 Preheat the oven to 400°F. Grease two cookie sheets. Roll out the light gingerbread mixture on a floured surface and use the two cookie cutters to cut out circles. Transfer these to the cookie sheets. Using the skewer, make a small hole through the dough about $\frac{1}{2}$in away from the edge of each cookie.

2 Bake the cookies for 10–12 minutes, until they turn golden around the edges. Immediately re-mark the holes in the cookies because they may have shrunk during baking. Transfer the cookies to a wire cooling rack.

light gingerbread mixture (see page 8)
icing and decoration
triple quantity of royal icing (see page 9)
blue, green, and red food coloring
fine blue, red, or green ribbon
equipment
2 cookie sheets
rolling pin
3$\frac{1}{2}$in and 3in round cookie cutters
metal skewer
wire cooling rack

paper for templates (see page 125)
paper piping bags
medium writing tip
plastic wrap
baking parchment
medium paintbrush
makes 12 large and 12 small baubles
baking time 10–12 minutes

3 Trace the bauble templates (see page 125) on to a sheet of paper and cut them out. Spoon a quarter of the royal icing into a piping bag fitted with the medium writing tip. Divide the remaining icing between three small bowls. Add blue coloring to one, green to the second, and red to the third. Thin each batch with a few drops of water until the icing has the consistency of thick pouring cream. Cover the tops of the bowls with plastic wrap to prevent a crust from forming.

4 Arrange the cookies in a single layer on the wire cooling rack and place a tray or sheet of baking parchment underneath. Position the large bauble template on one large cookie and pipe a line of royal icing on to the cookie, around the curved edges of the paper. Use the same technique on all the cookies, using the smaller template on the small cookies. Pipe a circle of icing around the skewered holes.

5 Place the red icing in a piping bag and snip off the tip. Use this to "flood" the top and bottom area of each bauble. Ease the icing over the sides with a fine paintbrush in order to completely coat the cookie. Leave to dry.

6 Place the blue icing in a piping bag. Snip off the tip and flood the central areas of each of the cookies. If

necessary, use a paintbrush to take the blue icing right up to the white, iced lines. Leave the cookies overnight to dry and set.

7 Pipe little triangular tree shapes on to half the cookies with white icing, and pipe a star at the tip of some of the trees. Pipe dots of white icing on the blue area around the trees. Pipe white, holly-shaped outlines on to the remaining baubles, with little circles for berries.

8 Put the green icing into a piping bag, snip off the tip, and use this to fill the tree and holly shapes. Ease the icing into the corners of the shapes with a paintbrush.

Fill the berry outlines with dots of red icing. Leave overnight to set.

9 Use more white icing to pipe over the initial template lines. Finally, thread the baubles with lengths of fine ribbon for hanging from trees or parcels.

TIP These cookies appear to take a long time to decorate because they need to be left overnight twice. This is to ensure that the colors do not run and to prevent the white from losing its vibrancy. However, the finished results are well worth the effort, making decorative baubles that outshine any commercial varieties.

Festive table centerpiece

This spectacular decoration makes a wonderful table centerpiece throughout the festive season. Pick the cookies from the tree as you enjoy after-dinner coffee.

1 Preheat the oven to 400ºF. Lightly grease a cookie sheet. Wrap the cardboard tube, which can be taken from an empty roll of foil or kitchen paper, in aluminum foil. Put more foil in the jelly roll pan, so that it loosely lines the edges, and lay the tube on top. Lightly grease the foil.

2 Roll out half of the light gingerbread mixture on to a floured surface. Using a sharp knife, cut out some simple leaf shapes, about 2in long and 1in at the widest point. Carefully mark a vein line down the

light gingerbread mixture (see page 8)

icing and decoration

double quantity royal icing (see page 9)

hazelnuts in their shells

dried apricots, prunes, or glacé fruits

silver-colored sugar almonds

confectioners' sugar for dusting

equipment

cookie sheet

cardboard tube

aluminum foil

jelly roll pan

rolling pin

sharp knife

2in star cookie cutter

wire cooling rack

metal or cane topiary cone, about 11in high and 8in across the base

11in board or plate

metal spatula

makes 1 gingerbread tree

baking time 8 minutes

center of the leaves with the knife, and transfer them to the greased cookie sheet.

3 Roll out the remaining mixture and use the knife to cut out out two small star shapes. (One star will serve as a spare in case of breakages.) Place the stars on the cookie sheet.

4 Cut out further leaves from the remaining dough, and arrange some of these leaves along the foil cylinder, so that they will bake in a slightly curved shape. Lay the remaining cookie shapes around the edges of the foil-lined tin.

5 Bake all the shapes for 6–8 minutes until they turn golden. Transfer the flat leaves to a wire cooling rack.

6 Wrap the topiary cone tightly in foil, tucking the ends underneath, and position on the plate. Use a metal spatula to spread a thick layer of royal icing over the surface of the foil.

7 Starting at the top, press the hazelnuts into the icing. Gradually work down and around the frame, creating a spiral carnival slide effect. Then press a row of dried apricots into the icing, next to the nuts. Alternatively, use prunes or glacé fruit.

8 Following the same pattern, press a row of silver-colored sugar almonds into the icing. Space the almonds equally between the nuts and apricots, as you work down and around the cone.

9 Use the cookies to fill the uncovered areas of the cone, overlapping them slightly at the tips. If they do not adhere immediately, apply additional royal icing to the frame and/or base of the cookie.

10 Secure the star to the top of the cone with a little more icing. Leave to set for at least 2 hours. Serve dusted generously with confectioners' sugar.

TIPS Do not make this decoration too far in advance if you are planning to serve it after dinner with coffee. This is because the cookies will gradually soften when exposed to the atmosphere. If you prefer, make the centerpiece up to three days in advance and wrap it loosely in plastic wrap to make an airtight seal and prevent the cookies from drying out.

A range of edible decorations can be used instead of the hazelnuts, sugared almonds, and dried apricots. For example, shelled walnuts, pecans, brazil nuts, prunes, dates, and chunks of crystallized ginger all look equally effective spiralling down the cone.

Festive skyscapes

These colorful, Middle Eastern–style cookies can be displayed on shelves, the dining table, or even as hanging decorations on the Christmas tree.

1 Preheat the oven to 400°F and grease a large cookie sheet. Trace the two templates on page 125 on to a sheet of paper and cut out the shapes. Roll out the dark gingerbread mixture and use the large template and a sharp knife to cut out ten shapes. If you plan to hang the decorations by ribbon, use a skewer to pierce holes through the top of the pieces, about ½in from the edge. (These holes will need to be re-marked after baking, as they are likely to close up slightly during baking.) Transfer the pieces to the cookie sheet and bake for about 10 minutes until the

dark gingerbread mixture (see page 8)

icing and decoration

royal icing (see page 9)

blue and gold food coloring

7oz red rolled fondant

confectioners' sugar for dusting

blue dragées

fine ribbon (optional)

equipment

large cookie sheet

paper for templates (see page 125)

rolling pin

sharp knife

metal skewer (optional)

wire cooling rack

paper piping bags

medium and fine writing tips

fine paintbrush

makes 10

baking time 10 minutes

dough has slightly risen. Leave the pieces on the cookie sheet for about 2 minutes before transferring them to a wire cooling rack.

2 Add blue coloring to half the amount of royal icing. Put the mixture in a paper piping bag fitted with a medium writing tip. Spoon the remaining white icing into a piping bag fitted with a fine writing tip.

3 Thinly roll out the red fondant on a surface lightly dusted with confectioners' sugar. Use the smaller of the templates and the knife to cut out the shapes of the buildings.

4 Scribble a little white icing across the base of one cookie and carefully lay the red rolled fondant buildings in position. Repeat this procedure for all the remaining cookies, each time gently smoothing the rolled fondant down with your fingers to eliminate any bumps.

5 Pipe a fine line of white icing around the edges of the buildings – pipe vertical lines across the red rolled fondant to separate each of the buildings. Also pipe decorative door outlines and windows in various sizes.

6 Use a small amount of icing to secure blue dragées on the roof tops and edges of some of the buildings. Use

more white icing to pipe plenty of stars in the sky above. Among the smaller "spot stars," pipe one or two larger star shapes at random intervals.

Pipe icing from the blue icing bag into the centers of the doors and around the edges of the skyscapes. Using a fine paintbrush, paint the roof and window details in gold coloring.

Put the cookies aside to dry. If you plan to hang the skyscapes as decorations, carefully thread fine ribbon through the holes. The pieces can be tied around the room and hung from window frames and mantelpieces.

TIPS These cookies also make attractive place-setting decorations for a Christmas celebration, in which case you might like to choose icing colors that match your own color theme. Alternatively, you could display a complete row along a shelf or mantelpiece. To make an upright row, secure several pieces together with icing and prop them up with small glasses or tumblers until they have set.

Gold dusting powder/petal dust/blossom tint can be used instead of gold food coloring, if you prefer. Mix it with a dash of clear spirit, such as vodka, to produce a liquid, paintlike consistency.

Decorated camels

These colorful camels, with their ornate reins, saddles, and feet, will be much admired during the festive season. Use a range of colors to brighten the room.

1 Preheat the oven to 400°F and grease the two cookie sheets. Trace the camel template on page 126 on to paper and cut out. Roll out the butter cookie mixture on a floured surface and cut out the camel shapes using the template (see overleaf). Put the template aside for use later on.

2 Carefully transfer the dough pieces to the cookie sheets making sure the legs remain straight. Bake for 6–7 minutes or until the edges turn golden. Leave aside for 2 minutes before transferring to a wire cooling rack.

butter cookie mixture (see page 9)
icing and decoration
royal icing (see page 9)
orange food coloring
2oz purple rolled fondant
2oz red rolled fondant
confectioners' sugar for dusting
colored dragées
small candies or colored
cake-decorating baubles
demerera sugar (optional)

equipment
2 cookie sheets
paper for template (see page 126)
rolling pin
sharp knife
wire cooling rack
paper piping bags
2 fine writing tips
plastic wrap
makes 20
baking time 6–7 minutes

3 Color half the royal icing orange and put it in a piping bag fitted with a fine writing tip. (If necessary, soften the icing with a few drops of water, as stiff icing can be difficult to pipe through fine tubes.) Put some white icing in another piping bag fitted with the other fine writing tip.

4 Thinly roll the red fondant on a surface dusted with confectioners' sugar. Cut out the blanket section of the template and use this to cut shapes out of the rolled fondant. Pipe a small amount of icing over the hump of each of the camels and secure the red rolled fondant, smoothing it in place with your fingers.

5 Roll out the purple fondant very thinly and use the knife to cut it into extremely thin strips. Secure the pieces to the camels with a little icing, to create the impression of reins hanging around the animals' heads and necks. Trim off the excess rolled fondant around the edges. It is best to work on a couple of cookies at a time, in order to prevent the icing strips from drying out before they can be put in position. (Keep the rolled fondant covered with a sheet of plastic wrap, which will help it to remain soft and pliable while you aren't using it.)

6 Press a dragée into each of the reins and decorate them with tiny dots of orange icing.

7 Use the white icing in the second bag to pipe a criss-cross decoration on to the blankets. Then use the orange icing to pipe tassels hanging down from the blankets. Secure dragées into the icing, while it is still soft.

8 Pipe lines of icing around the feet and secure small candies or baubles. Then pipe the eyes with a little orange icing. Leave the camels aside to dry for 2 hours, then store them in an airtight container for up to three days.

TIPS Although the camels look attractive arranged randomly around the table, they are more effective displayed in an upright position. Try propping them up against candlesticks or vases, or perhaps arrange them in a train along a shelf or dresser. For extra effect, you could create sand dunes using mounds of demerara sugar on a tray or board. Then, arrange the camels in a line along the surface, propping them up with wooden toothpicks.

The theme can also be expanded upon. A range of other animals, including horses or elephants, can in fact be made using a freehand or copied template. Indeed, any animal that is traditionally ornamented for festivities could be used to make stunning decorations for all kinds of events, not just Christmas.

Gingerbread nativity scene

This familiar stable scene is made entirely of gingerbread. Gold food coloring adds the finishing touches to this delightful nativity.

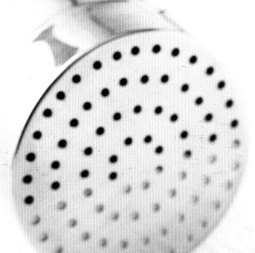

1 Preheat the oven to 400°F. Grease the two cookie sheets. Trace the nativity templates (see page 126) on to paper and cut out. Roll out the gingerbread mixture on a floured surface and use the templates and a sharp knife to cut out the stable shapes and characters. Transfer the cookies to a cookie sheet.

2 Reroll the remaining trimmings of gingerbread mixture. Cut out seven rectangles, measuring 2in x ½in, and three rectangles measuring ¾in x ½in, which will become the supports for the characters.

light gingerbread mixture (see page 8)

icing and decoration

1 tablespoon lightly beaten egg white

2 tablespoons cocoa powder

brown and gold food coloring

royal icing (see page 9)

½ cup demerara sugar

equipment

2 cookie sheets

paper for templates (see page 126)

rolling pin

sharp knife

fine and medium paintbrushes

wire cooling rack

paper piping bags

13in round or square flat plate

or gold cake board

medium writing tip

thin paintbrush

makes 1 nativity scene

baking time 9–12 minutes

3 Bake the pieces for about 7–10 minutes until they are just turning golden around the edges. Swap the cookie sheets around halfway through cooking.

4 While the cookies are baking, mix the egg white with cocoa powder to make a smooth paste. Brush the cocoa paste over the cookies in the areas shown on the templates, then return all the cookies to the oven for a further 2 minutes. Carefully transfer the shapes to a wire cooling rack.

5 Blend a small amount of brown food coloring into about a third of the royal icing. Put the mixture in a piping bag and snip off the tip. Pipe a small amount around the back and sides of the large stable section. Assemble the stable toward the back of the board, carefully securing the two side sections to the back piece. Use small glasses or tumblers to support the sections while they set.

6 Pipe more icing along the top edges of the stable and on the meeting edges of the roof sections. Carefully secure the roof pieces into place.

7 Place some white icing in a piping bag fitted with the writing tip. Use this to pipe the details on to all the characters. The shepherds have a simple outline and

headband, while the kings require crowns and robes. Use quick simple swirls for the coats of the sheep and remember to pipe around the edges of the star.

Thin the remaining white icing with a little egg white or water until it has the consistency of thick cream. Put the mixture in a piping bag and snip off the tip. Use this to flood the areas shown on the figures, such as the trim of the kings' robes. Leave to set overnight.

Paint gold food coloring over the piping on the star and kings with a thin paintbrush. Then lightly dust the top of the stable with cocoa powder. Next, spread a little icing

along two adjacent sides of the cookie rectangles. Place these iced sides against the board and the figures, so that the rectangles prop up the cookies in a vertical position. (Use the longer rectangles for the tall figures and the smaller ones for the shorter figures.) Scatter demerara sugar all around the cookies to finish.

TIP The gingerbread for the nativity can be baked and stored in an airtight container up to two days before assembling.

A few days after assembly, the cookies will start to soften, particularly if the scene is positioned in a warm place.

Templates

(All templates should be enlarged by 200%)

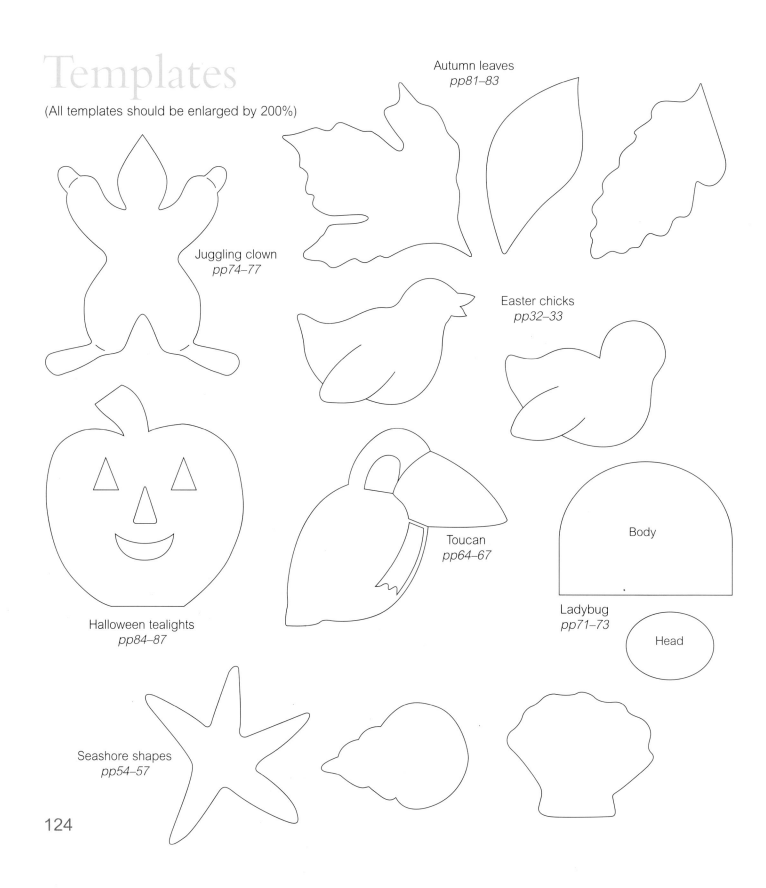

Autumn leaves
pp81–83

Juggling clown
pp74–77

Easter chicks
pp32–33

Toucan
pp64–67

Body

Ladybug
pp71–73

Head

Halloween tealights
pp84–87

Seashore shapes
pp54–57

(All templates should be enlarged by 200%)

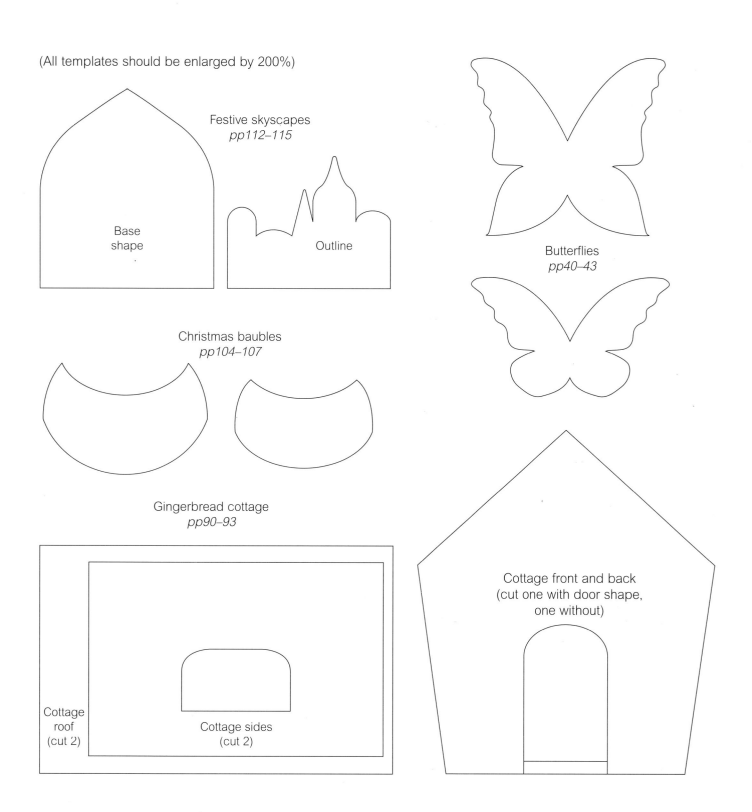

Festive skyscapes
pp112–115

Base
shape

Outline

Butterflies
pp40–43

Christmas baubles
pp104–107

Gingerbread cottage
pp90–93

Cottage front and back
(cut one with door shape,
one without)

Cottage
roof
(cut 2)

Cottage sides
(cut 2)

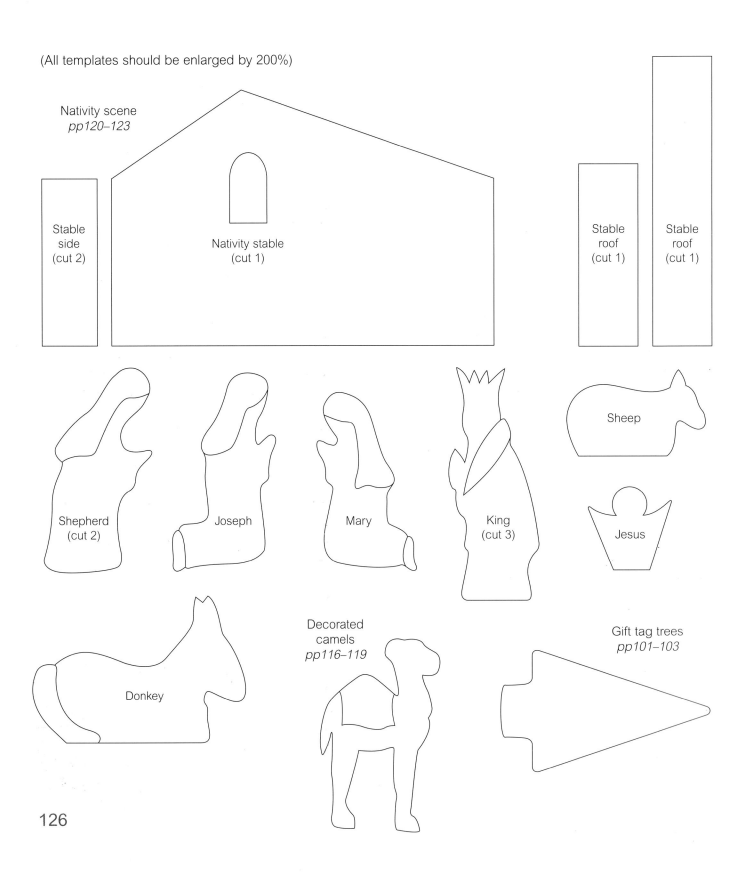

(All templates should be enlarged by 200%)

Nativity scene
pp120–123

Stable side
(cut 2)

Nativity stable
(cut 1)

Stable roof
(cut 1)

Stable roof
(cut 1)

Shepherd
(cut 2)

Joseph

Mary

King
(cut 3)

Sheep

Jesus

Donkey

Decorated camels
pp116–119

Gift tag trees
pp101–103

Index

List of suppliers

Most of the ingredients mentioned in this book are readily available at your local supermarket or cake-decorating supply shop. However, if you have trouble finding any of the decorating elements, you may want to contact one of the following companies, all of which specialize in baking goods:

American Cake Supply
522 North Halleck
Demotte, IN 46310
For a list of items carried in the store, browse their Web site at
www.americancakesupply.com.

Kitchen Krafts
1478 Elon Drive
Waterville, IA 52170
Either browse on-line at www.kitchenkrafts.com or call them (toll-free) at 1-800-776-0575 for a copy of their free catalog.

New York Cake Supplies
56 West 22nd Street
New York, NY 10010
Either browse on-line at www.nycake.com or call them at 1-212-675-2253 for a copy of their $5 catalog.

Sugarbakers
4800 Central Avenue Pike
Knoxville, TN 37912
Either browse on-line at
www.knoxplace.com/sugarbakers or call them at 1-865-689-6877 for a copy of their $5 catalog.

Sugarcraft
2715 Dixie Highway
Hamilton, OH 45015
For a list of items carried in the store, browse their Web site at www.sugarcraft.com.